Yale Bowl
and the
Open Trolleys

by

John D. Somers

DORRANCE PUBLISHING CO., INC.
PITTSBURGH, PENNSYLVANIA 15222

ISBN # 0-8059-3985-7
Printed in the United States of America

First Printing

For information or to order additional books, please write:
Dorrance Publishing Co., Inc.
643 Smithfield Street
Pittsburgh, Pennsylvania 15222
U.S.A.

Front Cover:

Our front cover is from the 1947 Yale-Dartmouth Official Program and was painted by artist Jim Fogleman. Since this was the last year for the trolleys, he ignored the usual cover, showing an Indian in trouble, and turned his attention to the trolley cars which have served the game-going fans so well.

Back Cover:

Car numbers 660 and 1460 represent the oldest and the newest type of open trolleys covered here. Number 660 was built in 1902 and was part of a group of cars built in 1901 through 1904 by the J. G. Brill Company. The 1400 series was the last order of opens and was built by Osgood Bradley in 1911. The cars ordered in-between these had railroad-type roofs. They returned to the monitor style with the 1400s and added roller type destination signs on each side and on the ends. *From the Ken De Celle collection.*

Contents

Acknowledgments

A special thanks to Kenneth F. De Celle of Springfield, Massachusetts, who encouraged us to write this story. He typed some copy on his computer, supplied several photographs from his negatives collection that were taken by the late Donald Shaw and Roger Borrup, and made some prints by himself. Without his help, it is doubtful that this book would have been made.

Other photographs are from Charles Brown, John Koella, my late brother Richard, and myself. Steve Conn of Yale University Sports Information and Betsy Herns from Public Affairs helped us.

About the Author

John D. Somers was educated at the Pratt Institute, having graduated in 1940 with a degree in mechanical engineering. Now retired he lives in North Haven, Connecticut. He is a member of the Shore Line, Connecticut, and Seashore Trolley Museums. Mr. Somers spends his spare time perusing every phase of his passion—trolleys, including history, models, and restoration of old cars. The delightful *Yale Bowl and the Open Trolleys* is his first published work.

Foreword

The city of New Haven, Connecticut, located on the north shore of Long Island Sound, was founded in 1638. It was a planned city with thirty-six squares or blocks, including a center green consisting of a four-block area. The green was not divided in quarters but in half, with Temple Street running North and South through the center. The western half was at a slightly higher elevation and was called the Upper Green, and the other, the Lower Green. The Lower Green faced Elm, Church, and Chapel Streets. Church and Chapel became the center or exchange place.

Because of its ideal location, the city grew very fast. By 1718 the first college opened and was named in honor of its principal benefactor, Elihu Yale. The college contributed to further growth.

Villages in the outskirts sprang up, bringing a need for public transportation. This was first furnished with horse-drawn wagons or omnibuses, but in 1860 a group of New Haven businessmen formed a horse-drawn railroad to serve Fair Haven in the east and Westville in the west. This helped to further develop the area. Thirteen other horse car companies were planned or in operation, but Fair Haven and Westville purchased or leased them all by the year 1900 and became the largest street railway system in Connecticut. West Chapel Street was the line of special interest here. This was a Fair Haven and Westville railroad line ending at Norton Street. After Yale College built Yale Field on Derby Avenue, the line was extended down Norton Street and out Derby Avenue to the field. The entire system was electrified in 1894-1895.

We have a map of New Haven, printed by the Price-Lee Company in 1901, which shows conditions as they existed a year or so earlier. The map shows the line going diagonally across the block that was later used for the Yale Field loop.

In 1901 Fair Haven and Westville received permission to build to connect with the Connecticut Railway and Lightnings line building east from Derby. The division point was in the town of Orange about one quarter of a mile west of Race Brook Road. The line paralleled the Derby Turnpike, but the tracks, which were on the south side, were far enough from the road so that carriage and auto traffic did not interfere with the trolleys.

The loop track at Yale Field and probably the third unloading track was built in 1903. Derby Avenue is on the town line of West Haven and New Haven. There was not enough room for the Yale Athletic Department to expand on the West Haven side because of an adjoining cemetery and the West River, so they looked to the north side of Derby Avenue to expand in New Haven.

Our 1901 map shows the area between Derby Avenue and Chapel Street to be developed. Except for some small parcels, the area from Central Avenue East to West River was obtained through the help of the city of New Haven. Except for where the loop track is, all streets were removed and Yale Avenue, which is not shown on our map, was built. To make room to build the Bowl was a large redevelopment project for its time. Our story covers the years from 1914, when the first game was played in the Bowl, until the end of trolley service in 1947.

The city of New Haven's population doubled from 86,045 in 1890 to 162,655 in 1930. This did not include area towns or Yale students, who are now counted. It has been in decline ever since. Chapel Street had a trolley run every few minutes. It was served by four routes plus the Derby and Waterbury cars.

One of the first electric cars, not a converted horse car, built by Jones in 1895. This ten-bench open number 289 has just left Church and Chapel. The dash sign reads WEST CHAPEL STREET-TO-NORTON STREET. This picture was taken after 1911 since a 1400 series Bradley is following. The car was scrapped in 1920.

Before the Building of the Bowl

The next five old photographs were taken after 1907, based on the dates the cars were built; our guess is 1908 or 1909. All the cars have single running boards, and Derby Avenue has not been paved. Double running boards were added to make it easier to climb aboard a car with the floor that was forty inches above the street. This reduced each step from about twenty inches to thirteen. It also made it easier for the conductor to collect fares and doubled the overload capacity from one to two lines of standees. Some of the cars were painted red at that time.

In the picture below, taken with Yale Field at the back of the camera, there are a considerable number of buildings across from the field. All these will be torn down to clear the land for the tennis courts and the Bowl. All the other four photos were taken from the other side of the street. The cars in the foreground, numbers 418 and 419, became 1137 and 1138; because they are so close together and have consecutive numbers, we believe that they are coupled in a two-car train. Train operation is explained later in this book.

Top: A Connecticut Railway and Lighting Company car from Waterbury with Providence fenders (the whisker-type people catchers).

Bottom: Former Winchester Avenue railroad car built by Jackson Sharp in 1899. It had Brill 22E Maximum Traction trucks and was scrapped in 1926.

Top: The knoll in the background was leveled and is the present site of the baseball stadium and field. The building was torn down.

Bottom: Car number 422 became number 1141.

Yale Bowl

We feel fortunate to obtain this aerial photograph of the Yale Bowl from the Yale University Office of Public Affairs. While taken four years after the trolleys stopped running, there is no noticeable change. The view is looking northeast. The intersection of Yale Avenue and Chapel Street is just above the Bowl. The visitor's side is above the field. The block of dark uniforms would indicate that the Navy game is being played. Note the empty seats which mark the division of reserved sections from general admission. General admission seating was started during the Depression. The field at the top of the photograph is in Edgewood Park which is not part of Yale. The light patch, north of the goalpost, is the Edgewood Avenue three-arch masonary bridge over the Park Drive and West River. Derby Avenue, where the trolleys were, is below the photo.

Yale Bowl
and the
Open Trolleys

In the 1880s, Walter Camp devised the game of football at Yale University in New Haven, Connecticut. At about the same time, Frank Sprague was credited with building the first successful trolley system in Richmond, Virginia. The trolleys soon became very popular, giving people a new, reliable, and inexpensive means of mobility they never had available to them before.

A trolley line was built up West Chapel Street in New Haven to Norton Street then south one block to the junction of Derby Avenue and George Street. The line then ran west along Derby Avenue to Derby and then to Waterbury. Yale University had a large tract of land on the west side of West River, where they built Yale Field.

The growth in popularity of football was tremendous. A committee of twenty-one men representing Yale and New Haven—or so the story says—debated for years at the start of the century about the need for a showplace for the university's football team that the city could eventually have.

When consent was reached, an architect named Charles Addison Ferry and the builder, John Sperry and Company, constructed Yale Bowl. They used 22,000 cubic yards of concrete, 470 tons of steel, and excavated 320,000 cubic yards of earth with a crew of 145 men for a cost of $750,000. It was the largest stadium in the nation just for football, with a capacity of 65,000 fans.

Opening day was for the Yale-Harvard game in 1914, which was a sell-out. The New York, New Haven, and Hartford Railroad added forty-three special trains of ten to twelve cars each to their already busy schedules. Trains brought fans from Boston via Providence, Putnam, Willimantic, Springfield, and Hartford. Other specials came from New York City and Poughkeepsie, in addition to many private cars. The open trolleys carried 33,000 to Yale Bowl. After the game, trains left New Haven Station every three minutes.

Yale was coached by Frank Hinkey, class of '95, and Alex Wilson was captain. The Yale team, called the Elis, had won seven of nine games that season but not the most important; Harvard won 36-0.

Yale officials soon realized that they had underestimated the size of the crowd that the Bowl could attract. They added another 15,000 wooden bleacher-type seats in the infield, increasing the capacity to 80,000. The attendance at the Army game in 1923 was 80,000.

The Connecticut Company also found that they had not provided enough feeders for the constant stream of trolley cars. Until more feeders could be installed, they ran as many two-motor cars as possible, even bringing some in from other divisions.

Yale Bowl is located on the corner of Yale Avenue and Chapel Street, about midway between Edgewood and Derby Avenues, so that the Edgewood line played an important part in moving the crowds. Open cars have been seen parked for five blocks from Alden and Fountain Streets and on to Dayton Street to Whalley Avenue. On Derby Avenue, it was double track, private right-of-way along the side of the road, west of Yale Bowl loop. Cars were stored on the east-bound track from Plainfield Avenue to the loop, a distance of one mile, while the Derby cars ran in both directions on the west-bound track. Also Yale Field loop, about equal to that of a city block, was filled with cars, as was a third track in front of Yale Field. According to John B. Judge, former superintendent of the Connecticut Company, there were 220 vehicles in action for the games. For some unexplained reason, ridership after the games dropped 10 percent.

I recall standing at the junction of Derby Avenue and George Street watching the starter with a switchbar route the cars in groups between Chapel and George Streets. The Chapel Street cars usually turned back at Church and Chapel and went back for another trip, while the George Street cars went to the railroad station. In later years, after George Street was abandoned, the railroad station cars turned down Temple Street.

Because of the large capacity of the Bowl, Yale could play most any team they wanted, and, except for alternating with Harvard and Princeton, all games were played at home. One of the teams that came every year was Army, with all the cadets. One year they decided to come by bus. The headline in the *New Haven Register* for November 1, 1925, stated very simply, WEST POINTERS NOT TO COME IN BUSSES AGAIN. The motor caravan carried 1,500 cadets. Many buses broke down and some even ran out of gas. Army went back to special trains after that!

In the 1920s it was very difficult to get tickets to the Bowl games unless you were a student or an alumnus. My father used to get tickets for a relative of ours. Attendance now runs 10,000 to 20,000, except for the Harvard games, which might draw 40,000 to 50,000.

When the Depression hit and things slowed down, the Connecticut Company's long-range plans included replacing the trolleys with buses. By the early 1930s the divisions which still ran cars became isolated. In the mid-'30s, about one hundred open cars were scrapped, including the fleet stored outside the West Haven car barn. The Edgewood Avenue and George Street lines were abandoned. Approximately eighty open cars were retained for football service, and, at about this time, aprons were installed in an effort to keep people from riding on the bumpers. The bleacher seats were removed from the infield, reducing the capacity back to the original 65,000.

In 1936 the Connecticut Company began express bus service from the railroad station, out Route 1 and down Marginal Parkway to the Yale Field. The fare was 25 cents in comparison to 10 cents or 3 for 25 cents on the trolleys. Even then it was still an impressive operation as related by the report of the chief engineer, Charles Rufus Harte's of the 1936 Yale-Harvard game:

The "out-of-towners" began to filter in, by rail, a day or so in advance, but the heavy train movement comes at the day of the game. Between 11:15 A.M. and the 1:15 P.M., twenty-four trains discharged some fourteen thousand passengers at the New Haven Station. In two-and-one-half hours, trolleys handled 14,800 passengers. Between 1:00 and 2:00 P.M., ninety-two trolleys passed the corner of Chapel and College Streets en route to Yale Bowl. [Cars made several trips.] This was in addition to the new express buses, which carried 3,200 passengers in 109 trips. Trolleys ran on a forty-five-second headway. In sixty minutes, the streetcars carried 12,300 passengers based on the fares collected. No doubt many rode free because it was impossible for the conductors to collect all the fares.

When the game was over, the open cars were all lined up to take the people back. I often watched them load. Most often people got on while the car was slowly moving, as you would an escalator. Within sixty minutes, ninety-five cars carried 12,300 passengers (fares collected). The bulk of the movement came in the first fifteen to twenty minutes, at which time cars carried 50 to 100 percent more passengers than the rest of the time. The streets of New Haven were back to normal in two hours while the trolleys were back to normal in ninety minutes.

At the 1936 game, 60,000 attended and a possible 10,000 used autos.

By this time other colleges had built large stadiums, and most of them offered full scholarships to star football players. The Ivy League colleges agreed not to buy players, and it is thought that this is the reason why Yale games have lost a lot of their popularity.

During World War II there was very little activity. Even the Harvard games were not played in 1943 and 1944. The chartered buses used to carry students to the field house, and the tennis courts were replaced with trolleys.

The Connecticut Company was under pressure from the federal government to move the open cars stored on the second floor of James Street barn to the outside so that the space could be used for manufacturing. The company argued that the old cars could not stand to be exposed to the weather, and without them there was no other good way to transport people to the Bowl when the war was over. The war ended before the company was forced to carry out the government's wishes.

In 1947 the Chapel Street line was converted to buses, but the line was kept serviceable for the trolleys' last football season. During recent years, thirty-one bad-order open cars had been scrapped. The shortage of opens forced some fans to use closed cars but most preferred to wait to get on an open car. By then a large percentage of cars were turned back at Church and Chapel Streets, and the cars were often filled before the crews had completed changing ends. The final day was Thanksgiving 1947, when New Haven and West Haven high schools played in the Bowl. When the game was over, the open cars had the long-unused dash signs and were routed to various destinations so that passengers did not have to change in the center of the city.

Open cars were discontinued in regular summer service when all lines went to one-man operation after the summer of 1927. The last lines to have opens were D, F, G, H, J, and M. This service required thirty-seven open cars, and an extra sixty-two opens were available. After regular open-car service was discontinued, the opens were used for special events only. During the Yale games, the opens operated in all kinds of weather. During a very heavy rain, attendance was down considerably and the company ran some closed cars. Young employees were used as conductors and the older employees as motormen. Even some retirees were called back for motorman duty.

D: Dixwell Avenue—Savin Rock via RR Station
F: West Chapel—Branford-Stoney Creek
G: West Chapel—Lighthouse
H: West Chapel—Momauguin
J: Whitney Avenue—Savin Rock via RR Station
M: State Street—Savin Rock via Congress Ave.

This huge movement of people was a very safe operation. There were few accidents. In 1925 a rear truck broke under a car at Norton Street and Derby Avenue. Within ten minutes, the car was removed, traffic resumed, and no one was seriously injured. A motorman was killed when he attempted to stop a runaway car which had lost its air and crashed into the car ahead. After that accident, the air was kept pumped up on the cars during the games.

At the end of the November 27, 1928, game, victorious Harvard fans ran out on the field and tore down Yale's goalposts. They carried parts on their shoulders. One of the sections, about twenty feet long and made of steel tubing four inches in diameter, was carried outside the Bowl by eight or ten men who carried it to Derby Avenue. As a trolley came past them, they hurled the tubing under the trolley, which narrowly escaped being derailed and crashing into another car going in the opposite direction. The tubing was so badly bent by the wheels that it curled up under the car. A long line of over fifty cars jammed with people were delayed outside the Bowl from 4:40 P.M. to 5:05 P.M.

How does modernization work? We now have the Wilbur Cross Parkway and Interstates 91 and 95. On June 6, 1993, the Bowl was used for the World Cup Soccer Game when the United States played Brazil. There were 44,579 people at the Bowl. The newspaper headline on the June 7 edition read, SOCCER FANS BRING I-95 TO A STANDSTILL. There were four accidents. Traffic clogged the streets and snarled traffic for hours, which lasted late into the evening.

As the Bowl approached its eightieth anniversary, it began to look shabby, but in 1994 each of the thirty portals leading into the Bowl were completely refinished, had new lights installed, and had their original gates painted and reinforced. There is a five-year master plan to prepare the Bowl for the twenty-first century, which could cost anywhere from $7 to $25 million and still awaits approval. The future for the Bowl looks good, but the open trolleys are gone forever.

An early crowd boards car number 1418 at Park Street for the Dartmouth game on October 19, 1940. There were several fraternity houses on this street. It is likely this group attended a pre-game luncheon there.

The Line Up During the Game

Ken De Celle (both)

Top: Looking east from Central Avenue, October 19, 1940.

Bottom: Looking west from Central Avenue toward Forrest Road. Notice the west-bound track in the foreground. The bus at the extreme right replaced the trolleys in 1937.

Ken De Celle

Looking West from the loop during the Dartmouth game on October 31, 1936, when attendance was 55,000, the largest since 1929. Notice the line of cars, down the hill towards Central Avenue, then up towards Forrest Road. The track was uphill to Plainfield Avenue and beyond. It was on this grade during the Brown game October 1, 1927, that car number 1434, which was first in line west of Forrest Road, lost its air and rolled down the hill. There was a space of one hundred feet or so left for free traffic flow on Forrest Road, so the car had a chance to gain speed and crashed into car number 1415. The bumper of 1434 went over 1415's bumper, so that it ran almost one-quarter the way through number 1415. This was the accident where a crew member lost his life while trying to prevent it. Car number 1434 was repaired and returned to service, but number 1415 was scrapped in March 1930.

Ken De Celle

This photograph was taken on October 26, 1935, during the Army game. Like many of these early pictures, it shows the cars before the addition of the aprons over the bumpers, which were added a year or so later. The cross-over in the foreground is where the Derby and Waterbury cars crossed over to the correct track after running east past the parked trolleys on the west-bound track. Car number 840 in the front of the line is still in service at the Connecticut Trolley Museum in East Winsor, Connecticut. The cars on the right are 1400 series and are on the third track. They appear to be moving West and could be going to Plainfield Avenue or into the loop. It is our opinion that it was planned in advance where each car would be parked during the game. Before World War II, the Connecticut Company did an outstanding job in organizing the movement of the trolleys for the football games. The building on the left is the Joel E. Smilow Field Center.

Ken De Celle

The above is a 1933 photograph of one of the Derby 1200s on its way to downtown New Haven. The Derby division ran these cars on what was called the "Hot Foot" between the two cities in the afternoons, in between the Waterbury 1900 series, to give fifteen-minute service. Having ridden both types of cars many times, it is our opinion that these were the fastest on the system. They were built by the John Stephenson Company, a Brill subsidiary, in 1907 and were originally assigned to Waterbury, where they ran on the Middlebury-Lake Quassapug-Woodbury line; to Thomaston; and one of the fastest lines in the state, the Cheshire-Mildale shuttle. They also ran to New Haven. Number 1206 was transferred to Derby between 1925 and 1932. They had Standard C-50 long wheel base trucks, designed for high speed service.

On the next page:

Number 834, one of the group built by J. M. Jones in 1905, taken on October 26, 1935, just after unloading its passengers in front of the Walter Camp Memorial.

Number 923 is at the upper level of James Street barn, ready to leave on a special for a game. One year newer than the above, it was one of the 900s to receive roll-type destination signs on the sides and both ends. This car has been restored at the Shore Line Museum, where the roll signs were removed.

Ken De Celle

John Koella

Looking east toward Yale Field.

The open cars had canvas curtains that could be pulled down in bad weather. Car number 1389 is identical to the 1400 in front except for the roof.

Car number 1127 was one of a group of Wasons which were equipped with multiple unit controls so they could be run in trains of up to three cars with one motorman. Note the coupler and the multiple pin connector (train-line coupler) below the headlight. This was the only car in the group to have Standard 050 trucks with four motors. The rest had Taylor SB trucks with two motors. The picture was taken on October 31, 1936, the day of the Dartmouth game. Number 1392 (behind) came from New Britain before 1934 and appears to be painted a different color. When the Connecticut Company was formed, the cars in the Hartford area were painted red with gold numbers, which might account for the difference. This car was one of the last to be scrapped in 1948 and was yellow at that time. On a tour through James Street barn in the '30s, we saw two Bradley open cars fresh from the paint shop. Surprised to see this at such a late date, we were told they wanted to have some nice looking cars for charter. This could have been done to cover the red paint.

Chas Brown (both)

Top: Army Cadet Band specials coming off the Viaduct onto Chapel Street with police escort.

Bottom: Before the rush starts at Church and Chapel Streets, both taken October 21, 1939.

Ken DeCelle

Car number 1429 has just passed over the switch on the crossover on the viaduct and will turn left onto Chapel Street on October 16, 1937, on the way to the Army game. This is the crossover where the Derby and Waterbury cars ended their run and turned back. The viaduct ran three blocks at street level, from Water Street to Chapel Street. In the days of rapid growth of the trolleys there was a need to double track State Street, but along this stretch the street was too narrow, so the viaduct was built on the edge of the railroad cut and behind the buildings on State Street. After the trolleys were taken off in 1948, the viaduct was taken down and was never used by buses.

In October 1936, the Connecticut Company started express bus service from the railroad station to the Yale Bowl. Don Shaw took this picture at 1:40 P.M. on November 21, 1936, the day of the Harvard game, at the station. Play was well under way at 1:40, which would explain the absence of people. Buses were first used on October 24 for the Rutgers game when only ten to twelve thousand were expected to attend. On October 26, two days later, the Edgewood Avenue trolleys stopped running. That line had already been running on single track between Howe and Orchard Streets for several months in preparation for repaving of Elm and Orchard Streets. This made the line no longer suitable to handle extra cars for the football fans. The route letter for Edgewood Avenue was Q. This was the first major line to be converted to buses. The Sylvan Avenue-George Street line, converted a few years earlier, was operated with single truck Birneys (four-wheel safety cars) with the route letter P and was lightly patronized. The buses to the Bowl took a different route than the trolleys, traveling out Columbus Avenue to Congress Avenue, thereby missing all the downtown traffic. The bus fare was 25 cents, 15 cents more than the trolley, but everyone had a seat.

New Haven Division Track Diagram

The track diagram on the next page shows the track that was in service as of December 31, 1927. Note the more direct route from Yale Field to the Railroad Station by way of George Street. All cars going to the games from the station had to go over the viaduct because there was no switch to allow the cars to go from Meadow to George Street. Cars going out Edgewood Avenue more than likely used Meadow Street.

This diagram has almost the entire New Haven system, with the following exceptions. There was a single track from the end of the Edgewood line, which is on Fountain Street, to Whalley Avenue on Dayton Street, which was used for storage of open cars during the games.

There was a single track from the viaduct along Water Street which had just been taken out of service. This was a loop line with the route letter R and ran on Water to East to Chapel Streets and over the viaduct. The summer of 1925 assignment sheet lists Car Number 801 for this service. This was the last single truck wooden car in regular service. It was modernized to be a safety car.

There was a single track on Temple Street between George Street and Congress Avenue and also at the end of State Street; the line turned down what is now Merit Street for one tenth of a mile to Scheutzen Park.

The trackage off Meadow Street was to the Silver Street yards used by the Connecticut Company's extensive trolley freight and express service. This was the fastest and cheapest way to ship over most of the state and took advantage of the nighttime hours, when passenger service was light or non-existent, to operate.

Track diagram from the Ken De Celle collection.

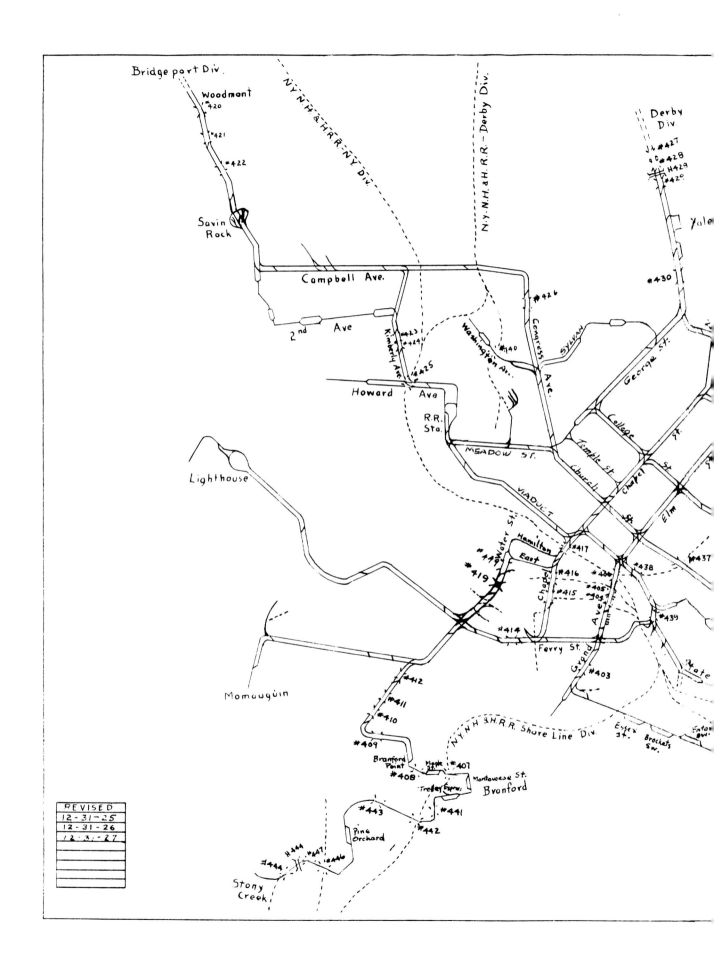

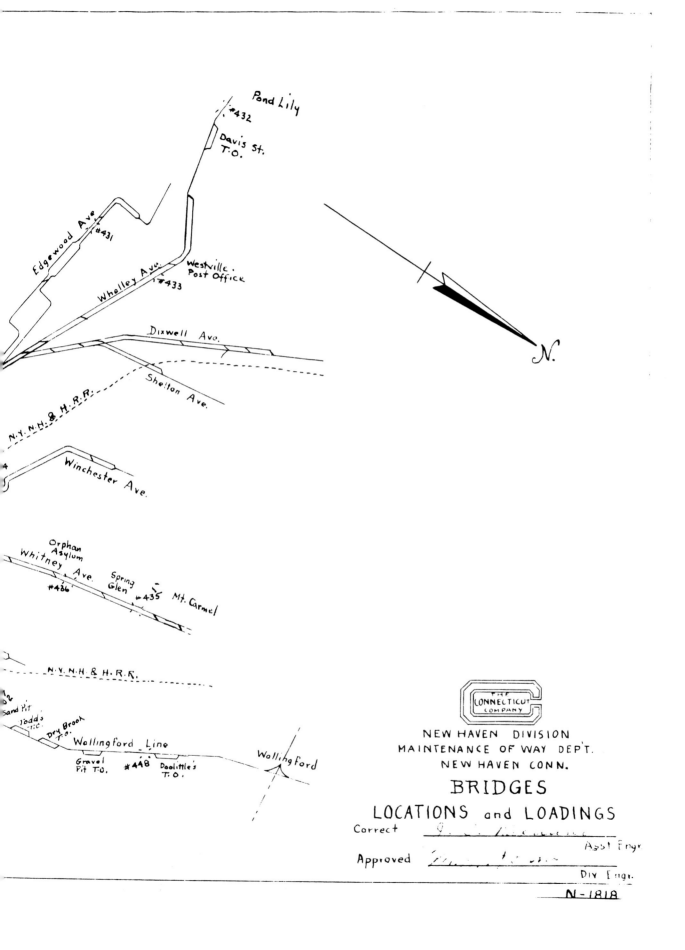

Pond Lily

#432

Davis St.
T.O.

Edgewood Ave.

#431

Wholley Ave.

Westville
Post Office

#433

Dixwell Ave.

Shelton Ave.

N.Y.N.H.& H.R.R.

Winchester Ave.

Orphan
Asylum

Whitney Ave.

Spring
Glen

#436

#435   Mt. Carmel

N.Y.N.H.& H.R.R.

Sand Pit

Todds
T.O.

Dry Brook
T.O.

Wallingford Line

Wallingford

Gravel
Pit T.O.

#448   Doolittle's
T.O.

N.

THE
CONNECTICUT
COMPANY

NEW HAVEN DIVISION
MAINTENANCE OF WAY DEP'T.
NEW HAVEN CONN.

BRIDGES
LOCATIONS and LOADINGS

Correct _____
                                    Ass't Engr.

Approved _____
                                    Div Engr.

N-1818

21

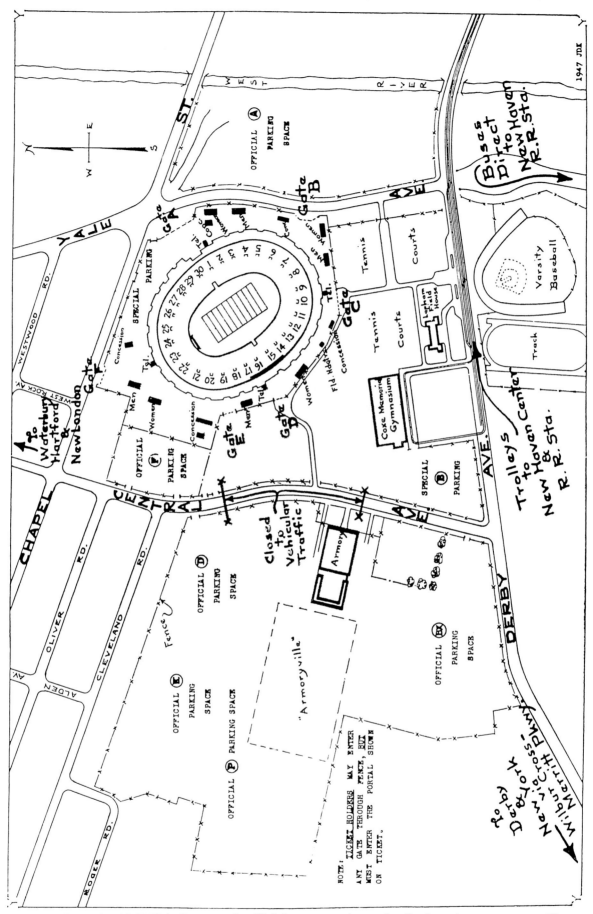

Map from the 1947 Yale-Dartmouth official program shows the final track arrangement. The rails West of the loop were removed so that Derby Avenue could be made into a four-lane highway.

The Last Rush

The last rush came at the Harvard game, November 22, 1947. Good attendance, the last chance to ride the trolleys to the Bowl, and the shortage of open cars caused the overloading.

John Koella (both)

Both photographs show the loading of car number 1423 at Church and Chapel Streets, before it had a chance to change over to the west-bound track.

John Koella

Motorman waits for a signal from the conductor to proceed west from Church and Chapel Streets. The bus, at the left, has replaced the regular trolleys.

John Koella

Looking east toward Temple Street.

John Koella

Looking east from College Street.

The building at right is the Hotel Duncan.
A few motorists did not avoid Chapel Street, but most did.

The photographs on this and the next page were all taken where the cars turned off Chapel onto Norton Street. We believe the car above must have carried the largest load of them all. A view of the other end of this car is on the bottom of page 28.

The kids yelled "Scramble!" and the riders would toss coins so they could watch them scramble for them. This is looking south on Norton Street.

Looking south on Norton Street, at the corner of Chapel. The string of open cars are returning to downtown for another load of fans. The lull in west bound traffic was caused by the shortage of open cars. Second in line is a 1900 series car built in 1919 by Brill. Except for the opens, these were the highest capacity cars on the system. They were for use in inter-city service and were used there until interurban service ended. Part of the sign hanger bar was removed to make room for an advertising poster holder, so the Yale Bowl sign had to be hung over the headlight. These cars faced early retirement but were instead given a major overhaul when World War II started. Because of this, they were still in good condition up until the end of the trolley in September 1948. Some were used to replace the regular city cars from which regular maintenance had been withheld.

After one game, my cousin and I boarded an open car at this corner. We found a spot on the running board, near the front of the car. Since the conductor started collecting fares in the front, when they left the Bowl, we expected to get a free ride downtown. Much to our surprise, the conductor worked down a crowded running board and collected our fare, which was 10 cents or three tokens for 25 cents.

Number 1429 has just turned from Norton Street onto Derby Avenue, which continues a block and a half East, behind the car where it emerges into Chapel Street. The street at the extreme left is George Street. The switches for this street were located about two hundred feet in front of the car. Note the peeled paint on the dash of the car has exposed the original number 463. When the Connecticut Company was formed, it took over the operations in eleven different cities, and each had its own numbering system. To get rid of this accounting nightmare, all the cars in the divisions connected by rail to New Haven were renumbered in 1915. Shortly west of the car was the Elsworth Avenue crossover. For many years, the Lighthouse (G), Momauguin (H), and sometimes the Branford-Stoney Creek (F) turned back here. The Ferry Street (E) also ran up Chapel Street and turned back at Norton Street, Elsworth Avenue, Yale Field and even went out to Plainfield Avenue, depending on the time. In later years the E replaced the L on Whalley Avenue. It is our speculation that the George Street cars also turned back at Elsworth Avenue before the track was connected from Sylvan along Whintrop Avenue to form a loop line about 1916.

BRILL OPEN CARS

Car No.	Date Built	Barn 1925	Barn 1927	Approx. Date Scrapped	Car No.	Date Built	Barn 1925	Barn 1927	Approx. Date Scrapped
612	1901	●	J	1939	737	1904	W	W	1935
613	1901	●	G	1930	738	1904	W	W	1937
614	1901	●	G	Note 1	739	1904	W	●	1935
615	1901	G	●	Note 2	740	1904	J	J	1936
617	1901	●	●	1930	741	1904	J	J	1947
618	1901	●	●	1930	742	1904	J	J	1948
656	1902	J	J	Note 3	743	1904	J	J	1948
657	1902	J	J	1948	744	1904	J	J	1947
658	1902	J	J	1936	745	1904	J	J	1947
659	1902	J	J	1937	746	1904	G	G	Note 5
660	1902	J	J	1948	747	1904	G	G	1937
661	1902	J	J	1937	748	1904	G	G	Note 5
662	1902	G	G	1937	749	1904	G	G	Note 5
663	1902	G	G	Note 4	750	1904	G	G	1937
664	1902	G	G	1948	751	1904	G	G	1947

JONES OPEN CARS

Car No.	Date Built	Barn 1925	Barn 1927	Approx. Date Scrapped	Car No.	Date Built	Barn 1925	Barn 1927	Approx. Date Scrapped
829	1905	●	●	1947	912	1906	W	●	1937
830	1905	●	●	?	913	1906	W	●	1947
831	1905	●	●	1947	914	1906	W	●	1947
832	1905	●	●	1947	915	1906	W	●	1947
833	1905	●	●	1947	916	1906	W	●	1937
834	1905	W	●	1947	917	1906	●	●	1947
835	1905	W	●	1947	918	1906	●	●	1947
836	1905	J	J	1930	919	1906	●	●	1937
837	1905	G	G	1948	920	1906	●	G	1947
838	1905	G	G	Note 2	921	1906	●	G	1947
839	1905	G	G	1937	922	1906	●	G	1937
840	1905	G	G	Note 4	923	1906	●	G	Note 1
841	1905	G	G	1948	924	1906	●	J	1947
842	1905	G	G	1948	925	1906	●	J	1947
843	1905	G	G	1947	926	1906	●	J	1934
909	1906	W	●	1937	927	1906	●	J	1937
910	1906	W	●	1947	928	1906	●	J	1937
911	1906	W	●	1947					

BARN: The barn from which the cars operated in 1925 and 1927
G = Grand Avenue   J = James Street   W = West Haven

Notes
1. Went to Shore Line Trolley Museum, East Haven, Connecticut.
2. Went to Seashore Trolley Museum, Kennebunkport, Maine.
3. Sold to James Melton Automobile Museum in Norwalk, Connecticut, and was placed in the open in front of the museum building. When the museum moved to Florida, the badly deteriorated car was scrapped and the trucks and hardware, etc., went to Shore Line Museum. The trucks later went to the Connecticut Trolley Museum.
4. Went to the Connecticut Trolley Museum, East Winsor, Connecticut.
5. Exchanged with newer, better conditioned 1400 series stored in the Stratford Avenue barn of the Bridgeport division about 1934. This is said to be done after service ended and just before the line was dismantled from Milford to Stratford.

Typical Brill open cars, number 741, built in 1904, is leaving James Street barn in the mid '20s. Car 656, built in 1902, is at Yale Field before the building of the Walter Camp Memorial. The seats and running boards have been changed for a trip downtown, but they are waiting for clearance to go to Plainfield Avenue to wait for the game to be over. The motorman is bundled up, so it is likely the last game of the season when temperatures could be below freezing.

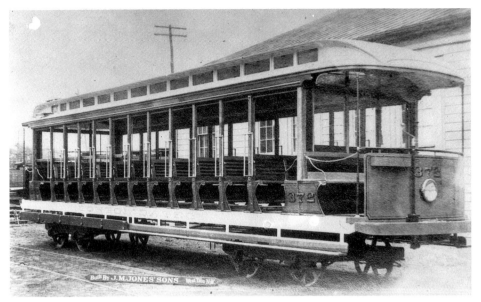

The start of number 372, the first order of Jones cars, would become number 829. Trucks and electrical equipment to be added in New Haven. The cars were lettered Consolidated before the Connecticut Company was formed.

The 900 series were the second order from Jones. Some of this group had roller signs added on the roof. These must have been the longest of them all, with every local as well as inter-city destination, such as Brigeport, Waterbury, Wallingford, etc. This 1920s photo was taken at James Street barn. Note the signal truck Birney behind number 925.

WASON OPEN CARS
Built in 1907

Car No.	Barn 1925	Barn 1927	Approx. Date Scrapped	Car No.	Barn 1925	Barn 1927	Approx. Date Scrapped
1100	J	J	1931	1133	J	J	1937
1101	J	J	1931	1134	J	J	1937
1103	J	J	1931	1135	J	J	1937
1104	J	J	1931	1136	J	J	1937
Note 6				1137	J	J	1937
1119	●	●	1937	1138	J	J	1937
Note 7				1139	J	J	1937
1126	G	G	1937	1140	J	J	1937
1127	G	G	1937	1141	J	J	1937
1128	G	G	1937	1142	J	J	1937
1129	G	G	1937	1143	J	J	1937
1130	G	G	1937	1144	J	J	1937
1131	J	J	1937	1145	J	J	1937
1132	J	J	1937	Note 8			

Notes

6. Four Brill cars, built in 1907, from Derby division with Brill 27G trucks, former New Haven-Derby Cars.

7. Former Hartford division, painted red when scrapped.

8. Car number 1126-1145 had multiple unit control and Taylor SB trucks, except 1127 had Standard 050 trucks with four motors.

The start of number 411 which became 1130 when renumbered. The photograph was taken at the Wason plant in Springfield, Massachusetts, in 1907. The trucks and electrical equipment will be added in New Haven. This is the first Connecticut Company paint scheme: gray roof, yellow sides to the floor, white with red running boards, and naturally finished woodwork. Note the alternate dark and light strips on the seat backs.

Car number 1143 ready to leave the lower level of James Street barn. Note the white sign, this indicates that it is an extra car to Winchester Avenue. The black sign under it shows it will then go to Savin Rock. We cannot explain the additional train connection on the roof.

BRADLEY OPEN CARS

1200 SERIES OPEN CARS

These cars were built by Osgood Bradley in 1910. None were originally assigned to New Haven, but some moved to New Haven after 1927 and were stored in the James Street barn for use for Yale Bowl service. All had Standard 050 trucks with four motors. All except 1278 and 1379 came from Bridgeport; those two came from New Britain.

Car No.	Approx. Date Scrapped	Car No.	Approx. Date Scrapped	Car No.	Approx. Date Scrapped
1252	1937	1261	1939	1265	1935
1253	Note 2	1262	1946	1266	1937
1254	1937	1263	1937	1278	1935
1257	1937	1264	1937	1279	1946
1258	1937				

This former New Britain division open car is leaving the James Street barn for a boat race special. Yale built a boat house at the west end of the Derby Division's track, along the Housatonic River, where the boat races were held a few times each spring. Riders also had a choice of getting off at the Derby railroad station and taking the train of bleacher cars or ride to the boat house where they could watch the races from the river bank. The train ran on the Shelton side of the river and stayed along side the racing shells for each of the several races. By the time the races were over, it would be getting dark, so the cars carried portable headlights, in this case a "Golden Glow," to get visibility in the areas where there were no street lights. At the time we rode the trolley and the train, we had a three-part ticket: one for the trolley to Derby, one for the train, and the other for the trolley home. At that time, in the mid-1930s, they used closed trolleys with one man, but the train was pulled by a steam engine.

BRADLEY OPEN CARS
Built in 1911

Car No.	Former Div.	Barn 1925	Barn 1927	Approx. Date Scrapped	Car No.	Former Div.	Barn 1925	Barn 1927	Approx. Date Scrapped
1387	M	●	●	1946	1435	NH	W	W	1948
1389	M	●	●	1939	1436	NH	W	W	1948
1390	M	●	●	1937	1437	NH	W	W	1948
1391	NB	●	●	Note 2	1439	N	●	●	1948
1392	NB	●	●	1948	1440	N	●	●	1948
1394	NH	J	J	1937	1441	SNB	●	●	1948
1412	NH	G	G	1948	1442	NB	●	●	1948
1413	NH	G	G	1948	1443	SNB	●	●	1937
1414	NH	G	G	Note 1	1444	NB	●	●	1948
1415	NH	W	W	1930	1445	SNB	●	●	1948
1416	NH	W	W	1946	1446	SB	●	●	1947
1417	NH	W	W	1948	1447	NB	●	●	1947
1418	NH	W	W	1947	1448	NB	●	●	1948
1419	NH	W	W	1948	1459	WD	●	●	1948
1420	NH	W	W	1947	1460	W	●	●	1946
1421	NH	G	G	?	1461	W	●	●	1948
1422	NH	G	G	1948	1462	W	●	●	1948
1423	NH	G	G	1948	1464	W	●	●	1946
1424	NH	G	G	1948	1465	W	●	●	1946
1425	NH	G	G	Note 1	1467	W	●	●	1948
1427	NH	W	W	1930	1468	WD	●	●	Note 2
1428	NH	W	W	1948	1470	W	●	●	1948
1429	NH	W	W	1948	1474	WD	●	●	1948
1434	NH	W	W	1948					

B = Bridgeport   D = Derby   M = Meridan   N = Norwalk   NB = New Britain
N = New Haven   S = Stanford   W = Waterbury

39

The Converters

In 1920 the Connecticut Company had more than four hundred open cars in regular system-wide service. To make it easier to collect fares, they decided to convert fifty open cars to pay as you enter—P.A.Y.E. They converted fifty of their best open cars. New Haven had twenty-four, Bridgeport six, and Hartford and Waterbury both had ten. This conversion involved closing in the sides up to the belt rail (about halfway from the floor to the roof) and cutting a twenty-three inch wide doorway in the end bulkheads. They also put three windows on each end but had no doors or other windows. Therefore, they were still open cars. The converters had new wooden seats, either cross-wise or longitudinal. One of the cars retained a sawed off version of the original seats with an aisle twenty-two inches wide along one side. The original running boards were removed, except for the door-opening at each corner.

With this arrangement, passengers were required to go aboard one at a time, pass by the conductor, and pay the fare. This made the cars no longer suitable for Yale Bowl service. The advantage of fast-loading open cars was lost. The capacity was cut from seventy-five to fifty seated passengers. It made things a lot easier for the crews when changing ends at the end of the line. The conductor no longer had to work the running boards, and it was better to be on a converter when a shower came up. They also were safer, since people used to jump off before the car came to a complete stop.

The converters were used on the State Street-Savin Rock (M) and the New Haven-Wallingford (C) lines and for shop extras. These cars proved to be very unpopular. As early as 1926, the rebuilt Standard 050 trucks and motors were exchanged with four Brill open cars in numbers 741 through 745. These along with four 600 series Brills replaced the converters on the State Street-Savin Rock line, and 700 series closed cars were used on the Wallingford line. The converters remained on the roster for extra service. They were all scrapped in 1930, except 1438 was scrapped in 1928. This could have been the one with the side aisle. The trucks and other parts were used to replace worn parts on other cars. All but three of the Brill opens still in service in 1947 had lost their Brill 27G trucks to Standard 050 from the converters. The cars retained the same numbers before and after the conversion.

Car No.	Barn 1925	Barn 1927	Car No.	Barn 1925	Barn 1927	Car No.	Barn 1925	Barn 1927
1393	G	G	1402	J	J	1410	J	J
1395	G	G	1403	J	J	1411	●	●
1396	G	G	1404	J	J	1426	G	●
1397	G	G	1405	J	J	1430	●	●
1398	G	G	1406	J	J	1431	G	G
1399	G	G	1407	J	J	1432	G	G
1400	J	J	1408	J	J	1433	G	G
1401	J	J	1409	J	J	1438	G	●

The only photographs of converters we have were not taken in New Haven but show the typical conversion. Number 1374 was taken in Bridgeport, while 1456 is in Waterbury. New Haven and Bridgeport divisions did not add safety screens on the side like 1374 has.

This three car special train of 1100 series open cars is ready to leave New Haven Green for Lighthouse Point Park in 1910 for the Edward Malley Company's annual outing. Malleys was one of the city's largest department stores. This is reportedly the last time they ran open-car trains. Lighthouse Point was a favorite place for picnics and outings. The multiple-unit control was much more complicated than the K-type used on the other cars and therefore more expensive to maintain. This is why they were retired fairly early. When open cars ran in trains, the people in the last cars had to cope with the dust kicked up by the car ahead. The only other cars that the Connecticut Company had that were equipped with train control, to our knowledge, was a small group of closed cars built for the Hartford-New Britain line in 1917 and the 200 series inherited from the Shore Line Electric in the New London and Norwhich divisions. All these cars were built by Wason.

West Haven storage yard in the mid-1930s.

Top: Looking south from Court Street. The barn is on the left.

Bottom: Looking north from Brown Street. The third car on the left is believed to
             be built by Cincinnati Car Company in 1906. Note the scissors type gate
             on the front platform. Most cars had a chain with a leather cover.

THE WALTER CAMP MEMORIAL. Inscribed on the two small panels on each side is, "Given by American Colleges and Schools uniting with the graduates of Yale to honor Walter Camp and the tradition of American College sport of which he exemplified." The large panels list the schools and colleges that contributed to the cost of its construction. It was dedicated in 1928, the same year the new stadium for Yale Field was built directly across the street.

Bibliography

Branford Electric Railway Journal (BERA) Fall 1988

Connecticut Co. Cars by Fred Bennett

Connecticut Co. Car Assignment Sheets summer 1925 & 1927

Electric Railway Journal 1920 via Traction Heritage Vol. 4 number 1
    and Vol. 7 number 2

New Haven Colony Historical Society Journal Vol. 29/no. 1 Winter 1982

Hegel, Richard and Shumway, Floyd. *New Haven: An Illustrated History.*
    Winsor Publications, 1981.

New Haven: An Illustrated History by Floyd Shumway & Richard Hegel

New Haven Register 10/12/25, 11/1/25, 11/28/28, 10/24/36, 11/17/89,
    6/7/92, 11/20/92, 6/26/95.

Richard B. Somers (my brother) trolley log book 1925-1927.

Trolley Days in Connecticut Nov. - Dec. 1983.

Notes from Ken De Celle

We believe this to be the largest standard open street car to ever operate in Connecticut and possibly anywhere in the nation, New York and Stanford had a few of these seventeen-bench opens for Rye Beach service.

About the Author

John D. Somers was educated at the Pratt Institute, having graduated in 1940 with a degree in mechanical engineering. Now retired he lives in North Haven, Connecticut. He is a member of the Shore Line, Connecticut, and Seashore Trolley Museums. Mr. Somers spends his spare time perusing every phase of his passion—trolleys, including history, models, and restoration of old cars. The delightful *Yale Bowl and the Open Trolleys* is his first published work.